The publisher gratefully acknowledges
the generous contribution to this book
provided by Charlotte Hyde and Jean Sherman and
by the General Endowment Fund of the Associates
of the University of California Press.

ENOLA GAY

NEW CALIFORNIA POETRY

EDITED BY

Robert Hass
Calvin Bedient
Brenda Hillman

For, by Carol Snow
Enola Gay, by Mark Levine
Selected Poems, by Fanny Howe

ENOLA GAY

MARK LEVINE

UNIVERSITY
OF CALIFORNIA
PRESS   Berkeley Los Angeles London

This work was generously supported by:
The Whiting Foundation;
the Council on the Humanities, Princeton University;
and the National Endowment for the Arts.

University of California Press
Berkeley and Los Angeles, California

University of California Press, Ltd.
London, England

Library of Congress Cataloging-in-Publication Data
Levine, Mark, 1965–
   Enola Gay / Mark Levine.
      p.   cm.—(New California poetry ; 2)
     ISBN 0-520-22259-8 (alk. paper).
     ISBN 0-520-22260-1 (pbk: alk. paper)
     I. Title.   II. Series.
PS3562.E8978E56   2000
811'.54—dc21   99-16316
                             CIP

Printed in the United States of America
08 07 06 05 04 03 02 01 00 99
10 9 8 7 6 5 4 3 2 1

The paper used in this publication meets the minimum requirements of
ANSI/NISO Z39.48-1992 (R 1997) (*Permanence of Paper*).

CONTENTS

ENOLA GAY

Then for the Seventh Night

Then for the seventh night in as many nights he strayed
into the vacant church and he kneeled in the aisle
with his hands in his shirt and he remembered the song
he wished not to remember; he remembered.
And he sang. And though the words were not familiar,

he kept singing, and he faced the dark altar
where among paint cans and tar paper
and a microphone with its wires torn out, he would have
lit a candle had one been provided.
But he had no gestures to give, only the song

whose disjointed verse he repeated. And he wondered
how many more nights his mission would last.
There was a magnet in his pocket and a hammer
in his pocket and he could hear bats or mice
or pigeons or maybe all three in the decayed choir loft.

He could hear the sound of the one train that came through
each night with its cargo rattling on rattling flatbeds.
He missed his mother. He would look for her still
in the green oblivious woods. And he would sing
the song that her long absence implied, though his voice

was not good and even he distrusted his voice.
From a nail hung a mural that he guessed was left behind
by migrant workers squatting in the church—
a brown field piled with thick red leaves
and in a corner the shadow of a figure.

He hadn't meant to go on so long. He hadn't meant
it. But the song would not go.
And the words no longer sounded like words.
Though he sang with his tongue behind his teeth.
Though he struggled to remove his hands from his shirt.

Eclipse, Eclipse

Sickness was near. All the gods knew it.
The air had been sprayed with the stiff sheen
of daybreak: a curtain fluttering; a window gone dim.
Not that the gods wanted it this way.
Their tent was cold, too. They knelt on the gravel
pondering the sky from which they long ago fell.
Who would carry the foul fumes away?
I kept an apple for Mother but ate the charred skins.

Comes a horseman, lazy on his mount,
helmeted in steel, rising from the pitted field.

How thick were the walls of the intimate crypt?
Thick as a pile. Thick as a blink.
I saw a fly buzz, saw it pirouette through rags of sky
ten thousand feet above the temple walls.
It came to a halt—it studied us—it was less hungry than we thought.
The rains persisted through morning, bringing rain,
the satisfaction of the third of three wishes.
Comes the wedding march, comes the onset,

Comes a horseman on unruly steed,
wounded through his heels.

The gods are not well braced. Their sleeves are
tattered and their flaring rockets
lie disabled by vandals.
Delay is all; all matrimony, plasma,
tokens of esteem, all vows exchanged in the cold heavens. . . .
The law is coming, three battered islands hence;
the splash is coming, the radar is coming, the law
is coming wearing Mother's private wig.

Comes a horseman, steady on the climb, a blade
against his thigh, a rumor on his spine.

Nearness is all. And the roots of the great tree
swayed in the heat, and the swollen seeds
struck the temple walls and left no stain.
Surely the great creeds could have warned us
to test the soil of nearby planets; our voices plunged
like the voices of the gods' outcast armies.·
All of us wanted to take the steep walk back
into the memorial noise; feeling sick, not feverish.

A pencil in his glove and a shovel in his soul
and big plans for a secret farm: comes a horseman.

Susan Fowler

The question seemed fair game to him, though the wind
was blowing strongly and the bearded man was speaking
too rapidly and the precise content of the question
could not be made out; but the question seemed fair.
He had asked himself the same thing not long ago.
Beyond the collapsed wooden fence

the red and black signs were too faded to read
but they might have been warnings; or they should have been.
He hoped the man would not inspect him for firearms.
An osprey was lunging at a pale blue heron in the marsh
and this was what he'd come to see, he thought,
but each time his gaze strayed past the man to the marsh

the man grew enraged. The man stood too close to him.
Was too visible. His beard three or four different
colors, his yellowed eyes beginning to water,
him wearing one shiny glove that ran up to the elbow.
Is there something wrong with this man? he thought.
The osprey's nest was rattling in the wind above them

on an abandoned telephone pole. He thought of a box:
a damp tin box. The man hit him on the chest
with a heavy stick, then a crop duster appeared

overhead with swirling lights. He could not see the pilot.
But he heard the pilot's voice, which he thought
was shouting "Come to bed" again and again.

Now he saw the man's name was "Susan."
The red stitching on the pocket of the man's
shirt said "Susan Fowler." The plane was gone. The heron
and the osprey were gone. He heard rifle fire
across the marsh. He wanted to laugh but could not decide
if laughter was an appropriate response.

Was it appropriate? Was it too soon to tell?
He thought to himself: "This man needs love."
And he offered the man his hand-tooled snuff box,
a sentimental piece behind whose every dent
there was a story. He thought he would never
leave this place. And for awhile he didn't.

Horizon

The Great War seen through a glass horse
balanced on a child's finger: the Great War
in the green, green bay; and the clock
on the mantel, and the frozen clouds.

Always the rousing black trumpets of the horizon.
The day was clear. The sky opened a dazzling lane
shaded by elms and by sundered willows.
We unloosed our gaze on the sea.

Almost late. Almost. Almost there.
Rose petals riding the salt-wave; hot tonic in search of land—
I had a vision of a trench and shared this vision
with my peers who typed it into the

"possibilities" file. It was the thirtieth day;
mystic symbols still a long way off. We prepared
our homes for darkness, the shuttered homes of our fathers.
A belief in progress

was general; progress in the acidity of the war-wrought soul.
The Great War seen from the reddest
constellation—the Great War seen through
the thread of my favorite trousers—the Great War

on the cusp of intelligence—the Great War clipped
by the feathers of a very angry bird.
Yes, and the sound of a little city burning.
Yes, and the sound of a child and a paper kite.

We hovered in the sky in a pool of fear,
a fear from childhood—capture and disposal
and rebirth: a sanded vanilla box set adrift
in the cool Asiatic waters in the next century.

Sadness. The ever-changing grasses.
The invention of prison. The crack in the
window that grows longer, not wider.
The sale of our invisible telescope.

Combinations

A basket of sand on silvered beach.
Red flowers in a square of moss.

Glistening scarves. A battered rosewood mask. Pale breeze.
Mallards in flight.

A plywood hut feathered with sawdust.
Ovals stamped in a clay box.

I have been unwinding wire from a spool.
Next I will sit at the loom.

Removing the lid to study marigolds.
Marigolds stuffed in her pockets like fists.

A blue arrow of painted logs.
A demonstration of games of chance.

White dog in my garden, white dog in their garden.
Winter above.

Jack and Jill

He galloped through the chill.
His purse rattling with pills.
On his tongue a desolate trill.
He pried a sack of rice
from a man with yellow eyes.
His name was Jack and Jill.

He clutched a steel device
against his ribs. It saved him twice,
once from x-rays, once from vice
and a woman. The land was ill.
His name was Jack and Jill.
His was a special case.

At dawn he scrambled pell-mell
through the woods to the shadowed rill.
He was hungry. Was he real?
Was he a rhyme? Was he a trace
of purple smoke escaped from base?
He'd taken a great spill—

he swallowed rain; he had a taste
of precious metals and malaise.
Is it easy to give praise
when his name is Jack and Jill?
He is rinsing his stained surface
with heavy water and a drill.

Counting the Forests

We had little to work with. That was his plan.
He was out until daybreak or nightfall or until
the reappearance of his servant who had fled
to the mountains during the ice storm.
He was out; he was out and his voice
was gone too. We heard streetcars scraping
down the hill outside his room; we heard drills
pressing the walls of the blue quarry.

He was counting the forests. That was his plan.
He carried a sack of dried fish
prepared by his servant and cured
in sea-salt. His servant was near; he could hear
the rasp of his servant's breath.
His servant was making the vigil in a mountain
somewhere in the ice-country; and the ice-country was vast
and blue and full of death-forms. So was the forest.

Here in the red forest: a forest of birds.
Birds and dark water and looming red leaves
brushed with murmuring voices.
They swept towards him, the voices, like tensed wings.
And he ran from them; but the red
forest was glazed and the trees were vast

with ice-forms. And at the edge of the red forest
he could see into the stone forest and could see

the voices rinsing over the stone floor.
He had been there already and had taken count.
And he had counted the animal forest and the
smoldering forest and the weeping forest and the forest
of the forgotten tropics and the God-forest.
What could he say to his accusers?

He set out in darkness. In darkness
we waited at the corner of the forest
for his reappearance. So many forests!
Somewhere was a silent forest. Ice above, ice below.
Somewhere was a coldness with a rope in it
like a memory-braid or a pair of braids.

Lyric

A new instrument slipped from the swinging shelf
and clasped in its blanched stem: daylight
—bringing to mind; bringing to mind—
and lodged in the mire among lost seed.
There went day.

Day passed. Day's cloud drew upon us
with its whistling machines leaning out for a sniff
and retreating. The women we hired
hauled wet sand from one mound to the next
in their flat shovels; not cautious; no;

examining the ridges of illuminated pests
lodged in them, their scarves, their headpieces.
I slanted atop my animal and watched
in the bristling rain. And when I could watch no more
I undid myself and watched.

A sick-room blossomed here once amidst the furred walls.
Two doors in; one door out;
the oil-bearing processions growing tangled
with insemination and then like migratory birds
staggering back to the weeds,

harm done and done.
I stayed put a long time getting to know that wall
and fed it scraps of breath and gained in return
a pinprick beneath my soul daily, twice daily, weekly.
Not for me only. A groping; an animal elegy.

My wall was spiked with
flowers whispering into the night, blue whispers,
eggshell, the maudlin unfurling and drying-out.
The sick left the sickroom; dropping
their white robes for shredding.

It was a model of passion. A flame-painting.
The grain of a so-called urge.
One eye disavowed what the other eye saw.
We sat there on the workbench with a jar of steaming fluid
there, in the theoretical fourth chamber.

Hello

1

It was time to learn a new word.
It was time to paste stars on the frosted window
to soothe the restless spirits.
It was criminal time. It was time to get his teeth
fixed by a friend of the family.
Time for charcoal. Time for clasps.

The fallen cedar blocked
his mother's closet and blocked his survey of the orange bark.
The suspicious orange bark. The suspicious stars.

2

"Coagulate." He sat on the bus across from a man
with a grandfather clock across the lap of his raincoat.
The man tapped his foot. The man had a thin
purple scar on one side of his nose.
The man looked at his watch and then looked at the clock.

The man said "This is my grandfather's grandfather clock.
He was a clockmaker. So was his grandfather.
He's in prison now. He thinks I'm dead.
He has lung disease. He'll go any day.
He's a hundred and four years old.

"There's something wrong with my blood," said the man.

3

It was time to learn a new number.
Is a number a word?
He took the bus to its last stop

on the edge of the desert and he ambled
through the desert to the assigned meeting place.

It didn't look like a desert. There were shrubs.
There were glass monuments and windmills and an open wagon
crowded with singing schoolchildren

and there were vacant guard towers painted like the sun
and there was a pipeline stained with birds.

A tree was burning, dressing the sky.
It was a kind of prayer and a kind of warning.

4

He reached the spot marked in the desert
by a bright red antenna. Eight or nine others
were already there. He greeted them.
He counted their pieces. He talked of old times.
He lay among them in sand, wrapped in sand,
waiting for the sun and for the music

that would follow the sun. "It's time," he said.
Was it already time? He scratched his watch.

5

His pointer was sore. He wanted to share
his experience with the public but the public
was hidden in boxcars. He examined a tree
and found nothing to report; branches, dried skin,
lazy stinging insects in a nest of wishes.
He wished someone would approach and put a coin

in him.
A phone was ringing and ringing.

6

"Hello," he said. "Hello hello."
It kept ringing at him

7

and he kept saying "Hello"
and he kept hearing voices calling back at him
repeating the familiar comforting threats

8

and he kept saying Hello hello

9

and this went on through the ruined night

10

the desert was swallowed by the ocean

11

the ocean struggled briefly and disappeared.

Lyric

At the very least.
Lines circulated. People and their braces, speech-flakes, dogged music.
Each signatory bearing a personal dye.
The row over a bag of stolen onions.
Timepieces reddened by wind.

I came whistling into daybreak
among marketplace skins and the poison shingles.
Another ferry collided with its version of fog
down there, in the dredged channel
by the unmarked cove. One more affront
to the one more who missed the last bell.
A love-variant. A spar always new.

That hat she waved at the mismatched pigeons—
gone too. She leaned her ladder against the wall
decorated with lavish molds, and climbed, and climbed.
I sampled an array of ices.
I sampled curds.
Take me to your place in your place, will you not?

Time found us sipping from the same cup.
A reflection was etched on the coal down there like a thumbprint.
Who doesn't love intrigue? Contagion?

They checked our bags and found a cotton wipe.
I had something to decline—an "inner glow"
that arced towards earth like a sex-shard.

It was lonely there. It always is, old man,
on the sandy beach in the rope collar of distant
generations. Winged shoulders and resolve.
First the parade. Then the crate. Then the fee.
Then the call to remnant arms.

The Response

Him again. Back from wherever he was hiding
or wherever he goes to draw attention
to what he's done. The screen door slams.
This time I didn't leave the light on for him.
I didn't leave his silver cup on the counter
by the sink. He roots around for the pills
on the night table; they're still there.

I'm still here. He must know I'm not sleeping,
I don't sleep when he's here. He grabs my
glasses from my face and puts them on and stands
above me, glaring down at me. He looks like me.
He looks a lot like me. Then he kneels down
and I know what's next. Later he complains

about the heat. I like it here with the windows
sealed, glazed and screened and sealed. When he came back
I was dreaming I traded a finger for a sack of meal
to feed the starving horses. I knew
he'd be back soon to stop the dreams.
He brought back money with him. That will help.
The tree out back is needing to be cut.
The trunk is crawling with red ants.
A few birds have died. Is there much else

to say to him? I can apologize.
I can take blame for what happened to him
though I wasn't there and I never believed
it was as bad as he claimed. But his face
did swell, and there were infections,
and he's still coughing,
that's all I can hear now, his coughing.

I'd like to tell him how I feel.
I'd like to think we don't have much time.
Each time I try to speak he finishes
my sentences for me in unexpected ways.
And he is right.

Place

There has to be a landscape-box for this—this—
sculpted oak-leaf braced in glass, oh pure-blown ash,
drenched chronicle anchored to a stem.
A box to sift the landscape from its pigments.

We were owing. We heard the high grass snap.
Competing shadows crossed us. Yesterday
I could have explained this better in the hallway
by the unlocked door in a broken hush. Yesterday
my soil slid towards you, you cradled
that thing wrapped in paper to your belt,
you were dutiful, that angle was permitted
and you waned.

I was wound up like a clan. My fixtures
receding into stonework with the antique carvings
of dogs and three-wheeled carts, ripe strands
of hay overspilling the edges. I called on the orange
tab to rid me of this shawl, its heaviness.
Its contamination. Its need to be bundled
into silence and tramped with shears
among the skewed roots of industrial hair.

My Friend

The woman turned when I whistled at her on the street.
I whistled in appreciation of her legs and ass.

"Were you whistling at me," she said.
"Yes," I said, "I'm sorry. I thought you were a friend of mine."

That was true. I thought she was a friend of mine.

She told me she had no friends. She told me
she was a theology student and was new in town.
She asked me what my friend was like.

I told her about my friend.
How my friend had been raised at a mission in the jungles
of Central America; how her parents had vanished one night
when the security forces raided the village;
how my friend had been held in a bamboo hut
blindfolded with a scarf; how she escaped
when she bit off the finger of a soldier who was raping her.

"Dear God," said the theology student.
I liked the innocence of that expression.

And then she told me her story.
And while she told me her story I watched a shiny
beetle crawling through her hair. I didn't know what to do

so I kept watching and when she finished her story
I said "Dear God."

She put her arm through mine.
"I've made a friend," she said.

She told me she could tell I was full of God.
"In a private way," I said, and she understood.
She said she would like to meet my friend.
"You can't," I said. "My friend's dead."

A Harvest

The ponies arrived: we were poised for absolutes.
Then a word—*arrows*; and a stiff-legged climb
to the toolshed of our elders, our betters;
there to minister endangered fluids

that still had the power to enchant.
Turning and turning our blades through living soil.

Pioneers we were. Often we found
a mule in the desert and offered it desert burial;
toiling to defeat the unclean grasses; to restore
to the landscape a missing color, like a scratch.

For the burial in the desert of the Hebrews is a fact.
And the burial of the pretenders, and of their songs.

Panic ascended and fled. One: the glad sight of a tree
bent towards the city with ribbons of illness
wound in its bark and in its inner layers.
Two: the harvest of eggs. Two: the harvest of perfection.

We sent for the girls for an evening of paternity and dance.
Mine had a big bellyache. The opaque waters turned

symbolic in evening's rust. I crawled beneath
my swayback mare and confided my misgivings.
Alone in the new snow with my clamp and my
pollution and an apprehension of love's chemicals.

Every decade a war song. Sometimes I feel like a (*what?*)
a child swaddled in eternal fabrics.

The glad sight of a tree grieving.
The glad sight of voices raised to the fatherless sky.
A train arrives from the city, seeking comfort
for its squawking cargo, and we turn the train away.

Two Springs

Toy soldiers on the windowsill in pools of glare.
The globes of Chinese lanterns strung from an alder.
A red scarf. A woodpile. A contest
between two springs.

And trying to wake no one
I climbed the stairs
of the wrong house
holding my shoes and stumbling on
the heirloom and there I remain.

I heard the click-beetles in the woodpile
reproducing wood. Once you told me about your mother
posed among the tinder
in her antique dress: your mother in the light of borrowed days.
Our plan (we were young and ashamed) was to
drown in the pond by the boathouse
while the leaves watched.

A peeling canoe stood there in the mud upright
in the divided Indian summer noon
like a stranded chapel, or not.
Each season the pond dropped lower, water

mixed with weed-killing acid, water poisoned
by the ink factory.

And the divers stayed down there, diving for coins
ashamed.

Twice I refused to visit your mother's
attic, but your mother would have it
no other way. She in her swimsuit
and red cap. Asleep and afloat
and the bathwater sticky with cold petals.

I went towards her as if pulled by a chain.
By then she had lost her gravity; and she softened
the air with blue kisses; and she sputtered
into the oncoming wave.

Ocean

What about the ocean? It was there
and it was there and he leaned towards it
and it stood upright like a sagging fence
and there was a horse in it. And a woman was

there, a green rag knotted in the ends of her
black hair, and she was pinning rough green sheets
to a clothesline in the ocean wind. Where was the
ocean? It wasn't looking at him and he tried

looking away but the woman dropped to the ground
or was blown to the ground and tiny white birds
scattered among the rocks like mice. And the mice
scattered too; and the ocean was ringing and he wanted

to get closer despite the flailing waves.
A desolate barge scraped the horizon
with its rusted hull jerking like a bell.
What was on the other side?

He got closer to the woman.
She must have been lying there a long time.
The water pushed through her and changed color
on the other side. The wind made a noise

like a scraping as it picked at what was left
of her. The green sheets had been replaced.
Though he tried to look away the woman's breasts had
been replaced, replaced by stone,

and her hair was tangled in the brittle stone,
and there were green bottles filled with sand
near the rotted fence post that hid the woman
from the ocean. And the ocean seemed

very far away and for a moment he thought
he smelled the resinous traces of the others
he had come to the ocean to get far away from.
The woman almost reminded him of the others

and the red insects that covered what was left
of the woman singed his leg and reminded him
of the others. The others would be finished
burning by now. A building stood in their place.

When he danced with the woman the woman appeared.
She pulled him to her. She pulled him under her.
They danced in the glare of the flailing waves.
She grabbed him by the mouth.

Lullaby

Nightfall. Falling night. Night and falling. Night. Night.
It brushed a smoke on his window. It twisted above him
like a bad toy. It stroked his broken ear, his broken hairy ear.
It lacked remorse.

The sea was a pressure. It could not be pleased.
Dangling him aloft on a sooty mattress.
Rinsing his sores with mist. His stunned needle
floating in hot alcohol in a jar.

Brine. Tweezers. Surrender. Rain.
On the avenue beneath the drenched sea-wall
he was made to contemplate the night time droning absence
of the mother-of-sky,

the mother-of-sea, the flying mother the wailing mother,
mother-of-stone, mother Asia mother cypress mother heat,
pilot mother, mother of song. And he called for her
and the sea had no remorse.

His paint can followed him through the night, the
threshold night, the stalled and laden night.
He remembered his mother's two names.
His paint can pinned him

to night's polished fuselage; and with paint-tipped fingers
he touched its hot sides, he touched its flaring dome.
He took instruction from the ocean spray and its voices
sang to him a lullaby.

And night drew him into sleep
across night's stiff salt-drenched smock.

Event

1. Thatched roof webbed against the sea.
2. Moon and red water, red sea-vines, sea-plants, the momentary shoreline.
3. Striped shirt knotted to the branch of a fir.
   Spotted shirt tacked above a sagging doorframe.
4. Darkness on one side; daylight beyond.
5. Rain. Glass tiles in a murky basin.
6. The instruction to dance, heels fixed to the plank.
7. Clattering of beads. Wind stirring the red lanterns.
8. ". . . a long way from home," etc.
9. Ladder angled against an angled wall; rungs blackened by bootprints.
10. Accordion, bamboo, crinoline, drift.
    Burial, crabgrass, demonstration, edge.
11. A metallic thrum beneath the pile of shavings.
12. "The women pretending to be crows,
    The men pretending to be something else."
13. Bodies glossed by moonlight.
14. A keepsake, a number, a means of transportation, a message, a rock.
15. Cudgel, dimension, effigy, guile, hasp.
    Effigy, guile, hasp, ink.
16. Asleep in the weeds with the migrating sea-birds.
17. Borrowing a stranger's varnished canoe.

Island Life

The noise approached us in a cube
with velvety forest bells hanging from a nail
and the noise was troubled by the scurrying of mice
and the noise was like. And the noise was like

Hunters arrayed with rope
and diagrams; or the birdlike demise of a dirty ancient tongue.
It hurt our ears; and dulled by rain we burnt
our soiled drapery one night in a dream, a dream

Altered, bilingual, depending: depending on the grandeur
of the gust hiding in our family war; depending on the sea.
In one hand I read a book called "I Remember Copper,"
swiveling my star from side to side. And in the other hand I.

I see my mother coming.
I see a people peeled like fresh envelopes.
Of course the noise abandoned us; and ever since I've stroked it
like a horse's leg, waiting for rain. Others stayed behind

Enjoying island life, vines and so forth, magnesium.
You must speak up to have your skin heard
inside the bristling cube. You must wear hot shoes
and speak up and speak with a universal stick.

Everybody

Today is everybody's favorite day of the week.
Everybody is rubbing ice across their necks and chests.
Everybody is visiting the gravesite of the President
leaving plastic cups filled with wine and chocolates.
Everybody is holding their breath as the song approaches its end.

And beneath the old rail bridge I run into a girl
I haven't seen in years, in a beautiful sun dress
stitched with colorful beads. It's a pregnancy dress: she says.
And we make love until the purple dusks on a pile of old tires
as the songbirds flutter above our heads.

This is the happiest moment of my life, I say.
And she says: this is the happiest moment
of everybody's life. And as we drift
down the river on a fallen log, others join us, drifting, singing,
and soon the dead and the sick and the poor are singing too.

And the stars begin to fall, and though everybody is waiting
for a terrible surprise, it hasn't come yet, not just yet.

Riddles of Flight

1

Mister gravity appalls me in his scarred closet;
here he has summoned me; here he mingles
his love-screeches with the sea. The sea is tempted.
The diving sea-birds dissipate like ballast.
Here I collide with splintered planks
of a remembered ship, oh far from home;

for my soul has been extracted by vicious means
and replaced by sod and by stirring eyesight.

2

Depredations of the nest
by unseen insects; the onslaught
of messengers; medallions swallowed like sugar;
a railroad bin consumed by potting soil:

Naturally the white horses followed
indecisions of the wind; one forded
an ice-crusted stream with a buzzard on its spine;
one toiled on the bank eating frozen reeds.

3

Even the sick-bell on her nightstand is gilded.
She spins like a siren; she has lost her *peanuts*
in the commotion of your visit. Open her up;
she's gone:
>   the consummation of ardent courtship.

And you who pace absently on her rug,
attending to sightings of land, below: be warned.
The ghost in the tree-top withdraws from your atmosphere;
she's gone:
>   the sea-chambers sealed with grass.

Lyric

A sentence delivered by nature
i.e. arriving cold, too late for snowdrifts or gratitude.
A picture painted: weeds
shrouding the sea-floor with braids of appetite.
We were hungry, too. Only less perfect.

Bag of justice. A stranger approached us
—always a stranger, always a sun-marred specter—
and with his fingers worked us with his prongs.
We were avid. Snapping our arrows in his dirt.
"Put a finger in me," we whispered at the high vantage point.

We whispered in the hedge-rows too,
and in the burial rooms beneath our flooded bins.
A ring of night-birds came down on the molded grains
and left hungry towards the sea to be touched
by salt. Evading judgment. Dispensing bands of weather.

He parked us in the marshy parts.
A sallow frontier. A bare spot like clay
on which his markings dimmed and were renewed.
We saw him push away on a waterlogged raft long ago.
The earth movers came for us then.

Enola Gay

It is many years after the fact.
I sent a squad to gather data
from the sticky asphalt, and they
are far away and very quiet. I do
wish I had not surrendered my wings.
I'm all out of seed.

And then through the pale red smoke of daybreak
I enter the garden—garden choked to its seams
with weeds and coiled roots and vines lurching
through the polished rose pebbles to the polished sky.
Can you hear the garden growing? Can you hear its motor?

Can you hear the crystal voices trapped beneath the growing?

Queen of the skies, pour forth your obsessing wrath!

2

They're having a clam-bake. With corn-on-the-cob.
With corn bread and clam juice and corn starch and clam skins.

They're having a clam-bake. They're baking my clams.
They're baking the clams pried from my steaming pond.

They're squeezing the lemon and biting the rinds.
They're plying the fire with red-veined kindling

snapped from the depths of the powdery grove.
They're burning the kindling. They're baking. They're dwindling.

Their spines are ringing. Their hooves splashed with fat.
They grow very small in the very red garden.

Cabbage at moonrise? Cabbage and air?
A mattress and a Jew's-harp and a vulgar stutter?

This year the trade-winds taste like butter:
butter and hunger, fear, sweet rain.

3

The craft is outfitted with smallish lacquered panels
where lights describe the blinking movements
of other prisoners. My screen is frozen.
I choose the Thimble, you choose the Horse, Mother the Shoe.
The messenger will drag behind him the Steam Iron.
And the black man? The black man is measuring us

from his shady perch above the electrical storm,
his finger limp on the device,
clinking "Yellow, yellow, yellow, yellow,
the stars be hid that led me to this *I*."
And I transmit a coarsely graven prayer.
And I disappear into the moist and comely

Oriental air,
and thence to tame my friend the broken bear. . . .

4

I am with child. With child again.
This time it's a child. This time it's a secret.

Shhh. The two of us; two of us and the sky.
At night I feel you whispering to me from your pouch,

startled by wind and vanquished windmills.
The sky is your father. So am I—

father and mother and severe mascot.
How ghostly your soul. I can tell by squinting.

I can tell by gazing with a mother's cruel black eyes
at your illuminated genes—genes spread out like spikes

in the star-heavy sky.
Reason be served; a thorn is growing in me from nowhere

like an idea.
It's marvelous. It's very big.

5

There stands a house under the mountain
of the world. Its floors are coal.
Its walls are hung with skins. Its dangling lamps
divide the obscene birds from the birds of the horizon.

There stands a house. Its horns are hewn
from stone and dying trees and wound with roots
seized from the polar garden. They are horns of love
and like the scalps of love they will be ground

into dust and sanctified.
Hear the bitter engines whine.
Hear the roll of royal dice.
Snake-eyes again, for the moment, and the next. . . .

Who is he we retrieve from the bunker?
He that is willing? He that empties the jungles?

—Yes; if the angry hammer agrees.
And I lead him for a tour of the clay pits at dusk:
he with the magic instrument, he
with the pierced wings, he in fancy,

he in fact. *The fact remains.*
Later we paused for a good cry and felt better.
I took a wrong turn and slid by candlelight
into the orphanage and faced the hero

in his cockpit. Here was no Negro.
His foot lay lodged in the barnacled steel trap.
He pecked at his ankle like a starved sea bird
until his teeth grew very tired.

Where can I drop you, he says.
Downtown Sumer, says I.

The Holy Pail

The holy pail. The mint of the colony.
The radiant fuel. The arrow. The wheel.
The bevel. The palm. The increase. The warp.
The tiller. The rut. The imaginary island.
The cathedral afloat. The prospering mercury.
The silo. The wish. The entrance. The rung.
The zero. The dome. The terminal carpentry.
The blighted soprano. The damming. The slack.
The hunting of mushrooms. The frozen instruction.
The breeze in the wardrobe. The silver. The silver.
The cracked archipelago. The eyesight. The law.
The pillar. The shift. The impeccable prey.
The valuable memory. The greed of the foliage.
The worry. The servant. The shovel. The like.
The emergency precinct. The motor. The milk.
The mother. The matter. The fabric. The fold.

John Keats

Here we were. Here here we were.
Graphite and plaster and cardboard and canvas.
A dozen human fingers of yellow rays.
Here fully exposed here fully protected.
Reclining like fresh-blasted stone, poised
here beneath the cracked canopy, clutching at flat planets,
adjusting the grains of light here
on our hair and throats.
The newly-dead were not lazier than we.
Our rings were melted for resembling rings.

Sleep had not touched us in however long.
The ill wind collapsed against the bole of the aspen
and could not reach us; and the hungry doves
thrashing above us were our shield
against the unverifiable rain.
                              Our ideal vase
was still with us; and as we passed it among us
the canopy changed in its mirrors—
changed to an arbor swelled with purple vines; changed to
a corridor of polished stone; to a silver pond
and silver moss; to a grove of coal-trees; to a chemical
grove. We plucked from the ground thick strands
of an ashy growth; and we saw in the veins

of the ideal vase blue boulders striking the walls
of the great city and pocking the avenues
of the great city. And we saw thunder
float above us in a spool of cloud.
                                        Our machine
was wired with forgetfulness and failed to ease
the pressure in our mouths, the pressure of the
ground in prayer. Our machine coaxed us
with half-messages from the dying system;
and we saw the machine was weak,
in need of rites; so we touched it with
leaves and with thistles and with dirt
and with a white flame and with uranium.
We touched it with sleep and we saw it
in a cloud uplifted on the wings
of nervous hawks. When would the great city
open itself to us? The ideal vase
recited to us treatment methods
we were eager to share.
                                        Our pilgrimage
is long and narrow and pitted with traps
scattered by man and by beast: mud; vipers; opiates;
virus; fallout. And the great city
is guarded by personal machines familiar
with suffering; machines with copper voices
high-pitched and trilling in the blank cold night.
Yes we have an offering to make to the earth.
Come here, and closer, and here, and here.
Our blue misleading box of soil

has grown crowded; crowded with ornaments
and with the anonymous powder of skeletons
and with laments.
We were sorry to hear of the earth's loss.
We send our regrets, burdens and regrets.

Lyric

Awash in the violated zone
in triangles of sun in a surgery bed. *In.*
Alerted through a twisting pipe. Fed from elsewhere.
Water running downhill underhill;
water loss.

I surrendered my copy. You surrendered my copy to you.
An envelope of eye-hair and milky paste.
Special glances traded through the tank of clouds.

Downstairs they were fitting flagstones
into the pegged outline of a path that wound
past the beehive to the fake pond.
Flagstones: gloss of an old world.
Our private crux. Hobble and hackle.
Reclining in our carriage when word got loose.
Bone-stew with beets served up in iron bowls.

Not that the signal for right response
was welcome. Two sailors blushed.
An incidental train slid from its harness.
Night-girl came to me with her bad hand

bent beneath the tray and would not leave night behind
until I rubbed beneath her skin with mine.

Seven-dollar fine. Twelve-dollar fine.
A signature in ink affirming—plus
stolen fixtures mended—plus bars of soap.
Ankle-rings. Tongue-clips. An incapacitating
serum in the stoppered cask.

The oak tree carved its initials in me
sheltering me from the waste-rain;
and the bare-armed girl with bruised wrists
stood there seething at the curb like a woman of sorts.
Like one who knew the whereabouts of my satchel
and its whereabouts.

Unlike Graham

Unlike Graham I can go on;
for I am attached to no particular
nurse, and unlike Graham I have salvaged
a wheel from the wreck of the fortress

and have hidden the wheel from public
display in a woolen envelope
stapled in the lining of my helmet.
Graham has no such luck; his scalp

is bare and glistens beneath
the lightbulb; and indeed there are arrows
sewn on his skull where they opened
him up to take a look. Oh Graham.

And now they have gathered in a circle
round Webber to pump him out
and take a look. What has Webber
to hide in his sorrowful pouch?—Not much;

they drop a few milky rocks in their tray
and move on. Webber was a fisherman;
he collected folklore; as a child
he lost an eye in a storm;

as a young man, like Graham, he
cannot go on. And I feel the wind
seeking me out; for the wind
has a light in it, like a chisel,

that wants to plant itself beneath
my helmet and grope towards the wheel
and from that corner capture the plea
that Graham hurls towards me as Graham wanes.

I would not give Graham's secret up.
Tonight I will sit in the window frame far from the nurse
down below; tomorrow too. For with Graham
going at the rate my wheel feels

him going, it is only a matter
of time, time, time, time, time.
I like the view here from the window
and the view likes me.

Winter Occasional

Stayed too long. Was made to see the thing.
Made to handle it, to scrape it clean.
The strain of heat. The wounded green
fabric, the thinking, the wan starling

crumpling into a stray eastbound train
in a flooded forest: Poland. Ice
in paper cups with sparkling juice.
Supper for two and two blue flames.

Then like a vapor, then like a many-
edged memory of the heroic clan:
the snow-queen descends, draped in a fan,
draped in a bone. She sees; she means—

wiping foam from the silver plate
on which she is melting. Is memory all
the hot discarded memory of a frail
voice, a specter, a desert, a height?

Mistook her hole for mine. Was bled.
Was made to pierce her tent with light.
The air was tilted at an awkward angle
and tasted, like lead, of the other side.

How Pleasant to Know Mr. Lear by Edward Lear

How pleasant to know Mr. Lear.
    Who was pulled from the heel of the tide.
He suffers from shingles and fear
    Of contagion—the moon—parricide.

His services do not come cheaply.
    His talents include excavating
And drilling and scavenging deeply.
    He kneels on the hot sewage grating.

Hear him tap at the windows of singers
    And beckon them break their harsh silence.
He kisses his nine crooked fingers.
    He inflicts on himself dreams of violence.

Night. The nine church bells are ticking.
    Mr. Lear winds a path through the alleys.
Have his wagons and gunboats been leaking?
    Has his purse filled with rain in the valleys?

The strays interrupt his reflections on
    Minerals. He sinks in his box.
He agrees that his odd predilections
    Justify the delivery of shocks.

Do you know of his skill with the crayon?
   Is his instinct for sums not appalling?
Have you studied the long cryptic essay on
   His burdensome prophetic calling?

How pleasant to know Mr. Lear.
   Who suffers who suffers from fear.
En route to the storm-battered pier.
   How pleasant to know Mr. Lear.

Forgetfulness

The bitter stalk was buried in me.
My boat swelled like a grape and kicked at the sea.
Great depths were suggested; a twisted tree
dragged past us on its sad current.

My claw offered no comfort. I wanted *results.*
A boy and his wounded mother read to me
in pleading tones from a history
of the human voice. I led them to a seat

on the rug and they fought
for a good view, despite their drifting eyes.
The bitter stalk was in me and I
cared what the yellow strangers thought.

They'd been brought here from some deep slot
in their ancestral land, summoned as if
by steam and ash, and now
they watched themselves shudder in the western

wind and grow confused among eager waves.
A good show. A show of mercy
that was tested long ago, prior to memory
and memory's incitements. Do you feel the aged craft

listing? It feels like the body of the woman I am told
I love. I love her. I need not worry
about the status of her flesh, for she
has been joined to the anti-matter. One more

stain to scrub from the wrinkled balance sheet,
one last lunge at the torn screen. . . .
My boat is thinking of me
and pointing at me with its steady

prow and biting its own splintered mast
like an unruly finger. Beware the dark sea.
What does darkness look like? What does it mean?
My bark is thinking of me, my unhappy bark

is balancing on its hook on the shaken sea
shrinking and sinking and blinking and thinking of the
distant blank blue hills. Where are my tall trees?

A Focus on the Elemental Oven (Six Moments)

Applause. Snapping of pencils in the hayloft.
Anxiety and its sullen child; the peek beneath a musty smock.
Firemen dancing with firemen, the scramble for a fist
of poppies, the sorrow, the restoration of nightfall. . . .

Ground was broken, a new kind of plank inserted
to offset the threat of seepage. Her hair was wet,
her hair glowed and white flowers were wound
in it and it must have been very hot in the garden.

Night was lavender. Night was approximate and plum.
I crouched beside the fence like a guilty pelt
counting frightened cattle as the guidebook recommends.
Fourteen, rocking chair, emphysema, sixty-three, testimony. . . .

A boy can get lonely. So can a girl. So can a girl.
Alone with a harness and a wounded gaze.
Alone in the bountiful archives, searching, soaked in oil
and negation and scoured with therapeutic soap. . . .

A shower of mustard, a tour of the windmills of Spain,
new lenses ground from clouded bottles and string.
The chimney falls and the burning continues and
what about the soot and whither the reinforcing agents?

The noble carpenters developed a syndrome
that was too big. I watched them suffer,
hammer and suffer, suffer and saw.
Until I had to borrow eyes to look.

New Song

It dawned on me. The sky; the white
and holy mud; the boiling stream; the thirst—
it dawned on me. It was dawn.
The evening's last horseman had trotted off.
My nets were full. Throughout
the fields my workers and my lovers
lay in a coiled ritual posture.
It dawned. In the silent fields it was dawn.
On horseback, dawn. The silver river slipped
off the mountains past my shadowed porch
into the frosted dawn at the edge of the fields.
Somewhere in the folds of daybreak lay the sea.
The river did not go unnoticed. The sick gray
gulls struggling above it did not go unnoticed.
For the sea was gone. The sea that flooded
my fields and drowned my wildest horses:
the sea. That sea. The yellow sea. The black and yellow sea.

Today the shrubs that twist along the marsh
are speckled with reddest berries. Late-summer dawn;
dawn filled with dawn, the lips and teeth and tongues
and swollen jaws of my lovers and my workers
mottled with berry-stains. They crawled in their thirst
from my fields to the berries. Berries like the sun,

exhausting to look at. Berries like the stars,
dark and fleshy and too beautiful to speak of
and incalculable. A shrike glances down
from the crisp pale horizon, it
seizes a cluster of berries with its spotted gullet
and returns squawking to its orbit
and falls to the fields to the aimless river-mud.

What invisible waters run beneath the dawn?
What secret destination can that bird have in mind?
My hungry white horse is afraid of the fires
in all directions; my horse is stumbling
towards the sea and the sea's obscure
resentful birds.

Jean Cocteau

We sang surrender and we sang defeat.
The bridges west of center and the tower
beyond the bridges empty in an hour.
A valley of steel and stone; a mist; a fleet
of barges, blank, unmoored, and in retreat;
nostalgic music (trumpets; viols); showers
of colorful debris. A white light scours
the ballrooms and dim cellars of the elite.

Little remains. A list of needs. Repair
to the arena and the colonnade
and clinic; and the memory of snow.

We tried installing with our tines a shade
of stolen green: and then we stopped; as though
astonished by the salt and random air.

Moon Mistaken

I

Elegance, and the rain-swept meadow
flecked with yellow, and the same half-remembered
lantern, and the soil. All for the sake
of the grainy tableau, murmuring, onwards.

This he drafted to Scholars who in the ill season
he trimmed as Soldiers. *This* he drafted to their mud.
And the poem passed through the sky in pursuit
of wounded heroes.

I implore: said the blades, whirling.
Jet fuel, blight, a wooden pillar
scissoring towards us through night's shallow rays.
The odds were grave. The need remained extreme.

And from our package—contents undesired—spilled
the silhouette, the tissue, the apron stained with memory.

2

Africa and the black wheel. A fleet of morbid
dreams seeking inland passage.

Asking: was it painful to wear the disguise
of dismantled ornaments? Asking the black blacksmith
and his bellows and his forge. He among the waters
who on the point of disappearance sings.

—And from the slanted scaffold a moonbeam
cast about like an anxious eye:
emptiness below; the cradle of blackness swimming
in a crescent of doubt, lacking fatigue, onwards.

Strategy. Silence. A fresh hot drought opened,
a residue of wind, an agriculture, a powder.
Dynasty and its green hunger were calculated;
and we strayed through the fortress like an illusion.

Chimney Song

Mother's shelf is crooked and bare.
Mother lost her hair.

We swim regardless. The white sandstorm
Is no cause for alarm.

Then in the plaza on coronation day
A shadow in disarray

Teased the hawks through the bare sky
Today; in disarray.

Wrapped in air in the absence of sun
We fell as one

And thought as one and sang or thought
We did; all for nought.

Mother's gash was tamped with pine-needles,
A nest of yellow pine-needles

Swept from the eaves of a wretched den.
But why and when?

Pilot came by with an illuminated book
And an injured rook; and the cook

Tried his best to deny what he'd heard,
Dusty forgotten lord.

All of our scalps itched all of the time.
The pollen's to blame,

And the stew and the wind and the wig and the sling
And the destination and the ashy thing.

Light Years

The failure to transport himself to the green green
woods—through the sun-raked hollows of the marsh,
through convolutions of bramble and desiring thorns—
was a chronic failure. And yet he loved the earth.

The birds of poetry, like paper birds installed
against a geometric fog, addressed
themselves to him in guilty hush, wanting
him, his sleep, his torpor, his signal, crest,

scenarios of daylight and of noise.
The little triangle that was his home withdrew,
blanched and withdrew in wind. Whose harshest fingers,
lit by glossy rings, strummed at his window now?

He was not alone. The fish of poetry,
teased from the cool white mud, eyed him always on their slow
ascent to the dawnlit surface; and the moon
crossing the water, anonymous hero,

was sent to incite him and remove him to
the woods where he would be almost alone.
He could smell the crumbling bloom of the acacia.
The night stammered through mist and moss and stone.

Once more he turned to the chronic water
looking for an end, and once more saw the watery
bent image of a plane dangling from clouds.

The Fixed Wing

Man in strictest uniform; man in daylight.
Man in ill-starred tunnel, upright, chirping.
Dutiful man, cupping the dusky paste of man
in a hollow rock; rock of man; rock.
Statue of horizontal man, slanted
on the bony tip of man, bronzed and wavering.
Man in field inspecting the knot
in a delicate plumb line. Man and his trigger.
Man's crown, man's hilt, man's gullet, the screech-owl
of man counting rings on a hot branch.
Man's eyes in disarray. Streaks of man
on the so-called horizon; man robed in garish
sunlight; ink blots, ferment, silver holster, dog,
the infirm lineage of ponderous man. Man of chance
swinging a woven sash beneath the arc—
beneath the bridge—beneath plumes of traffic.
Rumors of man and man's entourage: man mislaid
in the unattended vale. Man and the fixed wing
of man seeking penance in sea-foam; matrimonial man,
blistered shield of man. Man's carriage,
man's hood, man's bath in the sweet clay.
Man in the vault singing the widow's prayer.
The combination of man and man in weedy gardens.
Man's footprint in disrepair. Man at odds

with salt-water and with the urgency of atoms.
Orbiting man. Man undone. Man in pursuit of the eel.
Man gathering shards of the withered fossil record.
Credit to man, to the winnowed breath of man,
man's echo, man's stem, man's eager haunted remains.

Elegy (Terence Freitas)

In the pasture by the copper stream
he at dusk in rope sandals striding
came upon them in the wild grain
with checkered handkerchiefs across their foreheads
the three of them, two of them, bog of each one,
the three of them.
      The soil sent forth
its exhalations. Mist to moon.
The stream ticked on, the still stream.

He joined them in the cargo hold.
Their fixtures intact. Their pigments swaying
beneath the bluing domes of ice-chips
in their buckets, foot here, finger here,
swaying like a frozen cross-section
of sky among stiff reeds. The manifest
torn along its corrugations into wings.

It was the rainy season. Rain was next.
The vines in the hangar
shone beneath the awning of unreal flowers.
He ordered a cab which pulled up soaked
and in whose varnished grains he was

aligned. Pressed against the various mirrors.
Hands affixed with ribbons of duct tape.
Radio signals caressing his spike.

It was warm beneath the vehicle and the vehicle's
output. It wore a music
in its tangle, its pipes, hooded gowns, grievings.
It cut along the footpath through the pasture
fringed with wildflowers. Dread appeared
but would not release to the stream
dread's code or coda.

Lyric

Noontide. Clipped by the yellowing crest
of a leaper, wings adrift, flaming sprig,
pinch of worldliness. Admonished.

Clenched palate of the breaker, salted song.
Weed-killer wagon run aground
by white rock washed, no, purified,
with wave and wave of desert grasses.
A drumbeat, its shadow, was offered
to the slurry, and to the bed of dry matter
therein. Marksmen on call
in the fog-stubble.

It lurched against the attentive thread,
our lozenge, our noon. it murmured, it ached,
it clipped; a child with his
bamboo shroud through blue mud came wading,
through cold and opacity, into blue rain.
Ice-melt crowded out his footsteps.

We ate what we altered. Day broke

against us like a foreign plea.
A child fed his leaf to a dog
and followed the animal home.

And followed the animal home, home.
Followed the animal home.

Wedding Day

I

I have an appointment with elsewhere
I told the crater
which was filling with water and fragrant debris.
But that's just me.

All the impatient green bottles were pairing off,
a few stuffed with dainty Spanish galleons.
I doused my rag in silvery butane.
I had a picnic to attack: lamb chops; childhood.

Mine was a wedding of pipeline and pomp.
My bride pranced barefoot in the rime-dusted marsh.
She who sold me her eventual surrender
before losing herself in the blades.

She was a pristine evasive gesture.
She was a prissy evasive jester.
Troubled by a prolonged fondling
at the construction bin she called home.

2

A confidential grimace in the ditch.
A brass band with its mouthpieces removed.

She in dejection
swung in one hand her broken heels
at the stone altar and in the other
tugged her ringlets.

The turbulent breeze had found me
and asked me to slumber in its physicist's truck.
I liked trucks. And this one's treads
had been scooped of sand with a sparkling trowel.

3

One of the emotions not included
showed up on my fruit plate
like a seed but more like a listening
device. You've swallowed all

the mints, whispered my mate to me.
The mint with the imprint of a slave ship
and its masts and its slaves floundering at sea,
oh never to be reproduced.

Home: the chaff of stereotypical daylight,
potatoes in the closet, the waxy floor;
and squatting in shadows beneath the fuse box,
distracted by trumpets, my only lonely bride.

4

It was solstice inside the atom
and I took a stroll
to the sandy atoll
where I hired a girl for a whirl.

There was room for me inside her and her family.
She was swollen with particles of Emerson.
She had a packet of locomotive stamps
that she longed to sell me in the future.

This is the future I said and she with longing replied:
You sir have bought yourself a shiny train.

Designer: Barbara Jellow

Compositor: BookMatters

Text: 9.5/14 Minion

Display: Meta Book

Printer and binder: Rose Printing